30 minute
thai

p

This is a Parragon Publishing Book
This edition published in 2006

Parragon Publishing
Queen Street House
4 Queen Street
Bath, BA1 1HE, UK

Copyright © Parragon Books Ltd 2005

ISBN: 1-40545-745-7

Printed in China

Produced by the Bridgewater Book Company Ltd

Notes for the Reader
This book uses imperial, metric, and US cup measurements. Follow the same
units of measurement throughout; do not mix imperial and metric. All spoon
measurements are level: teaspoons are assumed to be 5 ml, and tablespoons
are assumed to be 15 ml. Unless otherwise stated, milk is assumed to be whole,
eggs and individual fruits such as bananas are medium, and pepper is freshly
ground black pepper.

Recipes using raw or very lightly cooked eggs should be avoided by infants,
the elderly, pregnant women, convalescents, and anyone suffering from an
illness. Pregnant and breast-feeding women are advised to avoid eating
peanuts and peanut products.

Contents

Introduction

Thai cooking is in many ways the ideal cuisine for contemporary living. It is intrinsically quick and easy, yet it looks great on the plate and offers a riot of fragrant and fiery flavors to tantalize the taste buds. What's more, it's healthy, based on a high proportion of vegetables and lowfat seafood and lean meats or vegetarian tofu. Also, stir-frying and steaming involve minimal fat or no fat respectively, as well as locking in the maximum amount of the foods' nutrients. And all this in 30 minutes or less! But to make things even simpler and speedier, here's a potted guide to stocking and using those essential Thai ingredients for the best, authentic results.

BANANA LEAVES Widely used as a natural wrapping for foods before they are baked, fried, or steamed. Soften in hot water if not pliable enough.

CHILIES Thai chilies are small and blisteringly hot, so handle with care and seed for a milder flavor.

CILANTRO The key fresh herb in Thai cuisine. Its fragrant flavor is more concentrated in the roots, so use these, scraped, if available, or the stems.

COCONUT A central ingredient used for flavoring and enriching both savory and sweet dishes. The milk comes in cans, and a reduced-fat variety is also available. Thicker, richer coconut cream now comes ready to use in cartons as well as blocks.

CURRY PASTE Thai curries are flavored with a spice paste, usually either red, from red chilies, or green, from green chilies and cilantro. These are available ready-made for speed and convenience.

GALANGAL A root similar to ginger but more intense in flavor, with medicinal-type undertones. Use fresh gingerroot if you can't find it.

4

JAGGERY A dark, coarse sugar made from sugar cane juice, perfect for adding a complex sweetness to savory dishes. Grate or cut pieces from a block.

KAFFIR LIME LEAVES These impart a fresh, fragrant citrus flavor. Finely shred the fresh leaves, which can be conveniently stored in the freezer, or use the whole dried leaf and discard before serving.

LEMON GRASS Its fibrous stems are wonderfully aromatic. If dry, soak in hot water first. Discard the outer leaves and chop the inner parts or bruise with the side of a heavy knife if using whole.

NOODLES Rice stick noodles (flat rice noodles) are widely used, the narrower kind in soups and salads, the wider in stir-fries. Soak in hot water before use.

PEANUTS Used toasted for garnishing noodles or salads, or ground in sauces—choose unsalted. Peanut butter provides a handy instant nutty boost.

RICE Jasmine rice is a fragrant long-grain rice that perfectly complements robust Thai flavors.

RICE WINE/VINEGAR Use sweet, aromatic Chinese Shaoxing rice wine and delicate white rice vinegar.

SHRIMP PASTE This has a concentrated, pungent fishy taste and aroma, which adds a hefty depth of flavor to fish dishes. Refrigerate after opening.

THAI FISH SAUCE An intensely savory, salty flavoring for pepping up all kinds of Thai dishes.

Soups & Appetizers

This red-hot relish is for all those devotees of the chili. It can also be served as an accompaniment to other appetizers, such as Crispy Pork & Peanut Baskets.

Hot Chili Relish with Crudités

serves 4

RELISH

8–10 large fresh red chilies, seeded and finely chopped

6 garlic cloves, finely chopped

½ cup water

½ tsp salt

2 tsp sugar

juice of 1 lime

1 tbsp Thai fish sauce

1 tbsp vegetable oil

SERVING SUGGESTIONS

carrot sticks

radishes

cucumber sticks

baby corn

Place all the relish ingredients in a pan and bring to a boil. Reduce the heat, cover, and simmer for 10 minutes.

Transfer the relish mixture to a blender or food processor and process until smooth.

Transfer the relish to a serving bowl and serve with a selection of vegetable crudités.

Using chili paste enables you to control the degree of heat in this dish, according to personal tolerance and preference.

Thai-Style Seafood Soup

serves 4

5 cups fish stock

1 fresh lemon grass stem, bruised and split lengthwise

pared rind of ½ lime or 1 dried kaffir lime leaf

1-inch/2.5-cm piece fresh gingerroot, peeled and sliced

¼ tsp chili paste, or to taste

1 baby leek

7 oz/200 g large or medium raw shrimp, shelled and deveined

9 oz/250 g (16–20) raw shelled scallops

2 tbsp fresh cilantro leaves

salt

finely chopped red bell pepper or fresh red chili rings, to garnish

Place the stock in a pan with the lemon grass, lime rind, ginger, and chili paste. Bring just to a boil, then reduce the heat, cover, and simmer for 10–15 minutes.

Cut the baby leek in half lengthwise, then very thinly slice crosswise. Cut the shrimp almost in half lengthwise, keeping the tail intact.

Strain the stock, return to the pan, and bring to a simmer. Add the leek and cook for 2–3 minutes. Season to taste with salt, if necessary, and stir in extra chili paste, if you like.

Add the scallops and shrimp and poach for 3 minutes, or until the scallops turn opaque and the shrimp turn pink and curl.

Drop in the cilantro leaves, ladle the soup into warmed bowls, dividing the shellfish evenly, and garnish the soup with red bell pepper or red chili rings. Serve immediately.

Tamarind paste and kaffir lime leaves add slightly sour and fragrantly citrus notes

to this lively soup, which contrast well with the sugar and sweet potatoes.

Spicy Thai Soup with Shrimp

serves 4

2 tbsp tamarind paste

4 fresh red chilies, very finely chopped

2 garlic cloves, crushed

2 tsp finely chopped fresh gingerroot

4 tbsp Thai fish sauce

2 tbsp jiggery or superfine sugar

5 cups fish stock

8 fresh kaffir lime leaves

1 large carrot, very thinly sliced

2 cups diced sweet potatoes

3½ oz/100 g baby corn, halved

3 tbsp coarsely chopped fresh cilantro

3½ oz/100 g cherry tomatoes, halved

8 oz/225 g large or medium raw shrimp, shelled and deveined

Place the tamarind paste, chilies, garlic, ginger, fish sauce, sugar, and stock in a preheated wok or large, heavy-bottom skillet. Tear the lime leaves and add to the pan. Bring to a boil, stirring constantly to blend the flavors.

Reduce the heat and add the carrot, sweet potatoes, and corn.

Let the soup simmer, uncovered, for 10 minutes, or until the vegetables are just tender.

Stir the cilantro, cherry tomatoes, and shrimp into the soup and cook for 5 minutes, or until the tomatoes have softened and the shrimp have turned pink.

Transfer the soup to a warmed soup tureen or individual bowls and serve immediately.

This speedy soup is a good standby, made in a matter of minutes using mainly pantry ingredients. If you prefer, you can use frozen crab sticks.

Corn & Crab Soup with Egg

serves 4

1 tbsp vegetable oil

3 garlic cloves, crushed

1 tsp grated fresh gingerroot

3 cups chicken stock

13 oz/375 g canned creamed corn

1 tbsp Thai fish sauce

6 oz/175 g canned white crabmeat, drained

1 egg

salt and pepper

TO GARNISH

shredded fresh cilantro

paprika

Heat the oil in a large pan, add the garlic, and cook for 1 minute, stirring constantly.

Add the ginger, then stir in the stock and corn. Bring to a boil.

Stir in the fish sauce, crabmeat, and salt and pepper to taste, then return the soup to a boil.

Beat the egg, then lightly stir into the soup so that it sets into long strands. Simmer gently for 30 seconds, or until just set.

Ladle the soup into warmed bowls and serve immediately, garnished with shredded cilantro and a sprinkling of paprika.

Brighten up your day with a bowl of this comfortingly creamy soup. The galangal adds a distinctive flowery aroma, but use fresh gingerroot if you prefer.

Chicken & Coconut Milk Soup

serves 2

1³⁄₄ cups canned coconut milk

scant 2¼ cups chicken stock

6 thin slices fresh galangal

2 fresh lemon grass stems, bruised

4 fresh kaffir lime leaves

8 oz/225 g skinless, boneless chicken breast, cut into strips

2 fresh red chilies, seeded and finely sliced

4 scallions, finely sliced

4 tbsp Thai fish sauce

2 tbsp lime juice

2 tbsp chopped fresh cilantro

Place the coconut milk, stock, galangal, lemon grass, and lime leaves in a large pan and bring to a boil.

Add the chicken, then reduce the heat and simmer, uncovered, for 10 minutes, or until the chicken is cooked and tender.

Add the chilies and scallions and simmer for an additional 3 minutes.

Stir in the fish sauce, lime juice, and cilantro, and heat through briefly. Ladle the soup into warmed bowls and serve immediately.

soups & appetizers

These crisp, golden-fried little mouthfuls are

packed with flavor and served with a hot-and-

Jumbo Shrimp Rolls with Sweet Soy Sauce

sweet soy dip—perfect to stimulate appetites at

the start of a meal, or as a tasty hot snack.

serves 4

DIP

1 small Thai chili, seeded

1 tsp honey

4 tbsp soy sauce

SHRIMP ROLLS

2 tbsp chopped fresh cilantro

1 garlic clove, finely chopped

1 tsp red Thai curry paste

16 won ton skins

1 egg white, lightly beaten

16 raw jumbo shrimp, shelled, tails left intact

corn oil, for deep-frying

To make the dip, finely chop the chili, then mix with the honey and soy sauce in a small bowl and stir well. Set aside.

To make the shrimp rolls, mix the cilantro, garlic, and curry paste together in a separate bowl.

Brush each won ton skin with egg white and place a small dab of the cilantro mixture in the center. Place a shrimp on top and fold over, enclosing the shrimp and leaving the tail exposed. Repeat with the remaining shrimp.

Heat the oil in a preheated wok or deep pan to 350–375°F/ 180–190°C, or until a cube of bread browns in 30 seconds. Deep-fry the shrimp rolls, in small batches, for 1–2 minutes until golden brown and crisp. Drain on paper towels and serve hot with the dip.

soups & appetizers

Use any inexpensive white fish for these fish cakes, since the other flavors are so powerful—frozen fillets, thoroughly thawed, would be fine.

Sweet-&-Sour Fish Cakes

serves 4

1 lb/450 g firm white fish, such as hake, haddock, or cod, skinned and coarsely chopped

1 tbsp Thai fish sauce

1 tbsp red Thai curry paste

1 kaffir lime leaf, finely shredded

2 tbsp chopped fresh cilantro

1 egg

1 tsp brown sugar

large pinch of salt

1/2 cup green beans, thinly sliced crosswise

vegetable oil, for pan-frying

SWEET-&-SOUR DIPPING SAUCE

4 tbsp sugar

1 tbsp cold water

3 tbsp rice vinegar

2 small, hot chilies, finely chopped

1 tbsp Thai fish sauce

To make the fish cakes, place the fish, fish sauce, curry paste, lime leaf, cilantro, egg, sugar, and salt in a blender or food processor and process until smooth. Scrape into a bowl and stir in the beans.

To make the dipping sauce, place the sugar, water, and vinegar in a pan over low heat and heat, stirring, until the sugar has dissolved. Bring to a boil, then reduce the heat and simmer for 2 minutes. Remove from the heat, stir in the chilies and fish sauce, and let cool.

Heat a shallow layer of oil in a large skillet over high heat. Divide the fish mixture into 16 balls and flatten into patties. Cook, in batches if necessary, for 1–2 minutes each side until golden. Drain on paper towels. Serve hot with the dipping sauce.

These tasty little appetite-teasers are an adaptation of a traditional recipe that uses a light batter, but phyllo pastry makes a good, easier-to-handle substitute.

Crispy Pork & Peanut Baskets

serves 4

4 sheets phyllo pastry, each about 16½ x 11 inches/42 x 28 cm

2 tbsp vegetable oil

1 garlic clove, crushed

4½ oz/125 g ground pork

1 tsp red Thai curry paste

2 scallions, finely chopped

3 tbsp crunchy peanut butter

1 tbsp light soy sauce

1 tbsp chopped fresh cilantro

salt and pepper

Preheat the oven to 400°F/200°C. Cut each sheet of phyllo pastry into 12 x 4-inch/10-cm squares, to make a total of 48 squares. Brushing each square lightly with some of the oil, arrange the squares in stacks of 4 in 12 small muffin pans, points outward. Press the phyllo down into the pans.

Bake the phyllo shells in the preheated oven for 6–8 minutes until golden brown.

Meanwhile, heat the remaining oil in a preheated wok over high heat. Add the garlic and stir-fry for 30 seconds. Add the pork and stir-fry for 4–5 minutes until golden brown.

Add the curry paste and scallions and stir-fry for an additional 1 minute, then stir in the peanut butter, soy sauce, and cilantro. Season to taste with salt and pepper.

Spoon the pork mixture into the phyllo baskets and serve immediately.

Morsels of chicken are wrapped in banana leaves before being pan-fried. These stylish little packages will set everyone's taste buds jumping.

Chicken Pan-Fried in Banana Leaves

serves 4–6

1 garlic clove, chopped

1 tsp finely chopped fresh gingerroot

¼ tsp pepper

2 fresh cilantro sprigs

1 tbsp Thai fish sauce

1 tbsp whiskey

3 skinless, boneless chicken breasts

2–3 banana leaves, cut into 1¼-inch/3-cm wide strips

corn oil, for pan-frying

sweet chili dipping sauce, to serve

Place the garlic, ginger, pepper, cilantro, fish sauce, and whiskey in a mortar and grind with a pestle to a smooth paste. Transfer the paste to a bowl.

Cut the chicken into 1-inch/2.5-cm chunks, add to the paste, and toss to coat evenly. Cover and let marinate in the refrigerator for 1 hour.

Place a piece of chicken on a square of banana leaf and wrap it up like a package to enclose the chicken completely. Secure with wooden toothpicks or tie with bamboo string.

Heat a shallow layer of oil in a large, heavy-bottom skillet over high heat. Cook the packages, in batches if necessary, for 8–10 minutes until they are golden brown and the chicken is thoroughly cooked, turning occasionally. Serve with a sweet chili dipping sauce.

Nobody will be able to resist these bite-size noodle-filled rolls served as finger food with drinks or as an appetizer, accompanied by a sweet chili dipping sauce.

Vegetarian Spring Rolls

serves 4

1 oz/25 g fine cellophane noodles

2 tbsp peanut oil, plus extra for deep-frying

2 garlic cloves, crushed

½ tsp grated fresh gingerroot

⅔ cup oyster mushrooms, thinly sliced

2 scallions, finely chopped

½ cup fresh bean sprouts

1 small carrot, finely shredded

½ tsp sesame oil

1 tbsp light soy sauce

1 tbsp rice wine or dry sherry

¼ tsp pepper

1 tbsp chopped fresh cilantro

1 tbsp chopped fresh mint, plus extra sprigs to garnish

24 egg-roll skins

½ tsp cornstarch

1 tbsp water

Place the noodles in a heatproof bowl, pour over enough boiling water to cover, and let stand for 4 minutes, or according to the package directions. Drain, rinse under cold running water, then drain again. Cut into 2-inch/5-cm lengths.

Heat the 2 tablespoons peanut oil in a preheated wok or large skillet over high heat. Add the garlic, ginger, mushrooms, scallions, bean sprouts, and carrot and stir-fry for 1 minute, or until just softened.

Stir in the sesame oil, soy sauce, rice wine, pepper, cilantro, and mint, then remove from the heat. Stir in the noodles.

Arrange the egg-roll skins on a counter, pointing diagonally. Blend the cornstarch with the water and brush the edges of 1 skin with the mixture. Spoon a little filling onto 1 pointed side of a skin.

Roll the point of the skin over the filling, then fold the side points inward over the filling. Continue to roll up the skin away from you, moistening the tip with more cornstarch mixture to secure to the roll.

Heat the peanut oil for deep-frying in a wok or deep pan to 350–375°F/180–190°C, or until a cube of bread browns in 30 seconds. Deep-fry the rolls, in small batches, for 2–3 minutes until golden brown and crisp. Drain on paper towels and serve hot, garnished with mint.

Noodles & Rice

Many Thai rice dishes are made from leftover rice that has been cooked for an earlier meal. The cooked rice is often stir-fried with a few simple ingredients and

Stir-Fried Rice with Egg Strips

aromatic flavorings, as in this recipe. If you have any leftover vegetables or meat, this is a creative way to use them up.

serves 4

2 tbsp peanut oil

1 egg, beaten with 1 tsp water

1 garlic clove, finely chopped

1 small onion, finely chopped

1 tbsp red Thai curry paste

2 cups cooked long-grain rice

1/3 cup cooked peas

1 tbsp Thai fish sauce

2 tbsp tomato ketchup

2 tbsp chopped fresh cilantro

TO GARNISH

fresh red chilies, cut into flowers

cucumber slices

To make the chili flowers, hold the stem of a chili with your fingertips and use a small, sharp, pointed knife to cut a slit down the length from near the stem end to the tip. Turn the chili about a quarter turn and make another cut. Repeat to make a total of 4 cuts, then scrape out the seeds. Cut each "petal" again in half, or into quarters, to make 8–16 petals. Place in ice water until the "petals" have curled back.

Heat half the oil in a preheated wok or large skillet. Pour in the egg mixture, swirling it to coat the pan evenly and make a thin layer. Cook until set and golden, remove from the pan, and roll up. Set aside.

Add the remaining oil to the wok, add the garlic and onion, and stir-fry for 1 minute. Add the curry paste, then stir in the rice and peas and stir-fry until heated through.

Stir in the fish sauce and ketchup and heat through briefly. Remove the pan from the heat and pile the rice onto a warmed serving platter.

Slice the egg roll into spiral strips, without unrolling, and use to garnish the rice, together with the chili flowers and cucumber slices.

noodles & rice

Basmati rice is cooked with creamed coconut, lemon grass, fresh ginger, and spices to make a wonderfully aromatic, fluffy rice.

Thai Fragrant Coconut Rice

serves 4–6

1-inch/2.5-cm piece fresh gingerroot, peeled and sliced

2 cloves

1 fresh lemon grass stem, bruised and split lengthwise

2 tsp ground nutmeg

1 cinnamon stick

1 bay leaf

2 small, thinly pared strips lime rind

1 tsp salt

1 oz/25 g creamed coconut from a block, chopped

2½ cups water

1¾ cups basmati rice

pepper

Place the ginger, cloves, lemon grass, nutmeg, cinnamon stick, bay leaf, lime rind, salt, creamed coconut, and water in a large, heavy-bottom pan and bring to a boil over low heat.

Meanwhile, wash the rice in several changes of cold water until the water runs clear.

Add the rice, stir well, then cover and simmer over very low heat for 15 minutes, or until all the liquid has been absorbed and the rice is tender but still firm to the bite.

Alternatively, bring the mixture to a boil, then cover tightly and turn off the heat. Set aside for 20–25 minutes before removing the lid—the rice will be perfectly cooked.

Remove the pan from the heat, add pepper to taste, then fluff up the rice with a fork.

If preferred, remove and discard the large pieces of spices and the lime rind before serving.

Jasmine rice is good enough to be served completely plain, with no other

flavorings. Here it has just the light tang of lemon and soft scent of basil.

Jasmine Rice with Lemon & Basil

serves 4

2 cups jasmine rice

3½ cups water

finely grated rind of ½ lemon

2 tbsp shredded fresh basil

Wash the rice in several changes of cold water until the water runs clear. Bring the water to a boil in a large pan, then add the rice.

Return to a rolling boil. Reduce the heat, cover, and gently simmer for an additional 12 minutes.

Remove the pan from the heat and let stand, covered, for 10 minutes.

Fluff up the rice with a fork, then stir in the lemon rind. Serve scattered with basil.

This colorful rice dish makes a meat-free meal in itself, with the inclusion of tender-crisp stir-fried vegetables and lightly cooked egg. Fresh Thai basil, available from

Egg-Fried Rice with Vegetables & Crispy Onions

Asian markets, has a more powerful flavor and fragrance than ordinary or "sweet" basil, with an interesting overtone of anise.

serves 4

4 tbsp vegetable oil

2 onions, sliced

2 garlic cloves, chopped

2 fresh red chilies, seeded and chopped

4 oz/115 g mushrooms, sliced

2 oz/55 g snow peas, halved

2 oz/55 g baby corn, halved

3 tbsp Thai soy sauce

1 tbsp jaggery or brown sugar

few fresh Thai or ordinary basil leaves, plus extra sprigs to garnish

3 cups cooked long-grain rice

2 eggs, beaten

Heat half the oil in a skillet over medium–high heat, add the onions, and cook, stirring frequently, for 10 minutes, or until golden brown and crisp.

Meanwhile, heat the remaining oil in a preheated wok or large skillet, add the garlic and chilies, and stir-fry for 2–3 minutes.

Add the mushrooms, snow peas, and corn and stir-fry for 2–3 minutes. Add the soy sauce, sugar, and basil, then stir in the rice.

Push the mixture to one side of the wok, pour the eggs into the bottom, and cook, stirring, until lightly set. Stir into the rice mixture.

Serve the rice topped with the onions, garnished with basil sprigs.

This dish features chicken and vegetables cooked together, and then served on a bed of rice mixed with cilantro and bok choy to form a delicious combination.

Chicken with Cilantro Rice

serves 4

2 tbsp vegetable or peanut oil

1 red onion, chopped

2 garlic cloves, chopped

1-inch/2.5-cm piece gingerroot, peeled and chopped

2 skinless, boneless chicken breasts, cut into strips

4 oz/115 g white mushrooms

1¾ cups canned coconut milk

2 oz/55 g sugar snap peas, trimmed and halved lengthwise

2 tbsp soy sauce

1 tbsp Thai fish sauce

CILANTRO RICE

1 tbsp vegetable or peanut oil

1 red onion, sliced

3 cups rice, cooked and cooled

8 oz/225 g bok choy, torn into large pieces

handful of fresh cilantro, chopped

2 tbsp Thai soy sauce

Heat the oil in a preheated wok or large skillet and sauté the onion, garlic, and ginger together for 1–2 minutes.

Add the chicken and mushrooms and cook over high heat until browned. Add the coconut milk, sugar snap peas, and sauces, and bring to a boil. Let simmer gently for 4–5 minutes until tender.

Heat the oil for the rice in a separate wok or large skillet and cook the onion until softened but not browned. Add the cooked rice, bok choy, and fresh cilantro, and heat gently until the leaves have wilted and the rice is hot. Sprinkle over the soy sauce and serve immediately with the chicken.

Perhaps this should be more correctly named

"drunkards' noodles," as it's a dish that is

supposedly often eaten as a hangover cure—the

Drunken Noodles

fiery kick of the chilies wakes up the system

and the aromatic lime leaves and basil cleanse

and refresh the palate.

serves 4

6 oz/175 g wide rice stick noodles

2 tbsp vegetable oil

1 garlic clove, crushed

2 small fresh green chilies, chopped

1 small onion, thinly sliced

5½ oz/150 g lean ground pork or chicken

1 small green bell pepper, seeded and finely chopped

4 fresh kaffir lime leaves, finely shredded

1 tbsp dark soy sauce

1 tbsp light soy sauce

½ tsp sugar

1 tomato, cut into thin wedges

2 tbsp shredded fresh Thai or ordinary basil leaves

Soak the noodles in a bowl of hot water for 15 minutes, or according to the package directions. Drain well and set aside.

Heat the oil in a preheated wok over high heat. Add the garlic, chilies, and onion and stir-fry for 1 minute. Add the pork and stir-fry for 1 minute. Add the bell pepper and stir-fry for 2–3 minutes.

Stir in the lime leaves, soy sauces, and sugar. Add the noodles and tomato and cook, stirring, until heated through.

Sprinkle with the shredded basil. Transfer to warmed serving plates and serve immediately.

An alternative to classic dishes such as Pad Thai Noodles, this quick and easy dish

is very filling.

Noodles with Mushrooms

serves 4

8 oz/225 g rice stick noodles

2 tbsp peanut oil

1 garlic clove, finely chopped

¾-inch/2-cm piece fresh gingerroot, finely chopped

4 shallots, thinly sliced

1 cup sliced shiitake mushrooms

3½ oz/100 g firm tofu (drained weight), cut into ⅝-inch/1.5-cm dice

2 tbsp light soy sauce

1 tbsp rice wine

1 tbsp Thai fish sauce

1 tbsp smooth peanut butter

1 tsp chili sauce

2 tbsp toasted peanuts, chopped

shredded fresh basil leaves, to serve

Soak the rice stick noodles in hot water for 10 minutes, or according to the package directions. Drain well and set aside.

Heat the peanut oil in a pan. Add the garlic, ginger, and shallots and stir-fry for 1–2 minutes until softened and lightly browned.

Add the mushrooms and stir-fry over medium heat for another 2–3 minutes. Stir in the tofu and toss gently to brown lightly.

Combine the soy sauce, rice wine, fish sauce, peanut butter, and chili sauce, then stir into the pan.

Stir in the rice noodles and toss to coat evenly in the sauce. Sprinkle with peanuts and shredded basil leaves and serve hot.

This simple, fast-food dish is sold from street food stalls in Thailand, with many and varied additions of meat and vegetables.

Hot-&-Sour Noodles

serves 4

9 oz/250 g dried medium egg noodles

1 tbsp sesame oil

1 tbsp chili oil

1 garlic clove, crushed

2 scallions, finely chopped

2/3 cup white mushrooms, sliced

1 cup dried shiitake mushrooms, soaked in boiling water for 30 minutes, drained, and sliced

2 tbsp lime juice

3 tbsp light soy sauce

1 tsp sugar

TO SERVE

shredded Napa cabbage

2 tbsp shredded fresh cilantro

2 tbsp unsalted peanuts, toasted and chopped

Bring a large pan of water to a boil. Add the noodles, return to a boil, and cook for 4 minutes, or according to the package directions. Drain well and return to the pan. Add the sesame oil, toss well to coat, and set aside.

Heat the chili oil in a preheated wok or large skillet over high heat. Add the garlic, scallions, and white mushrooms and stir-fry for 2–3 minutes until softened but not browned.

Add the shiitake mushrooms, lime juice, soy sauce, and sugar and bring to a boil, stirring. Add the noodles and toss to mix.

Serve the hot noodles spooned over Napa cabbage, sprinkled with the cilantro and peanuts.

This is the best known of all Thai noodle dishes. Inevitably, there are variations on the basic dish—for instance, diced firm tofu is often used instead of pork.

Pad Thai

serves 4

8 oz/225 g wide rice stick noodles

2 tbsp vegetable or peanut oil

2 garlic cloves, chopped

2 fresh red chilies, seeded and chopped

6 oz/175 g pork fillet, thinly sliced

4 oz/115 g raw shrimp, shelled, deveined, and chopped

8 fresh Chinese or ordinary chives, snipped

2 tbsp Thai fish sauce

juice of 1 lime

2 tsp jaggery or brown sugar

2 eggs, beaten

¾ cup fresh bean sprouts

4 tbsp chopped fresh cilantro, with extra to garnish

¾ cup unsalted peanuts, toasted and chopped, plus extra to serve

crispy fried onions, to serve

Soak the noodles in a bowl of hot water for 10 minutes, or according to the package directions. Drain well and set aside.

Heat the oil in a preheated wok or large skillet over high heat. Add the garlic, chilies, and pork and stir-fry for 2–3 minutes. Add the shrimp and stir-fry for 2–3 minutes.

Add the chives and noodles, then cover and cook for 1–2 minutes. Add the fish sauce, lime juice, sugar, and eggs. Cook, stirring and tossing constantly, until the eggs are just set.

Stir in the bean sprouts, cilantro, and peanuts and heat through briefly. Garnish with cilantro leaves. Serve with accompanying small dishes of crispy fried onions and extra chopped peanuts.

This tasty dish combines sweet and sour flavors with the addition of egg, rice noodles, colossal shrimp, and vegetables for a real treat.

Sweet-&-Sour Noodles

serves 4

3 tbsp Thai fish sauce

2 tbsp rice vinegar

2 tbsp superfine sugar, brown sugar or jaggery

2 tbsp tomato paste

2 tbsp corn oil

3 garlic cloves, crushed

12 oz/350 g rice noodles, soaked in boiling water for 5 minutes, or according to the package directions

8 scallions, sliced

6 oz/175 g carrot, grated

1¼ cups fresh bean sprouts

2 eggs, beaten

8 oz/225 g cooked shelled colossal shrimp

½ cup ground unsalted peanuts

1 tsp dried chili flakes, to garnish

Mix the fish sauce, vinegar, sugar, and tomato paste together in a small bowl.

Heat the oil in a preheated wok or large skillet. Add the garlic and stir-fry for 30 seconds.

Drain the noodles well and add to the pan with the fish sauce and tomato paste mixture. Mix well to combine.

Add the scallions, carrot, and bean sprouts to the pan and stir-fry for 2–3 minutes.

Push the mixture to one side of the pan, pour the eggs into the bottom, and cook, stirring, until lightly set. Add the shrimp and peanuts and stir until heated through. Transfer to warmed serving dishes and serve immediately, garnished with chili flakes.

Sesame seeds and oil bring a pleasing texture and a sweet, nutty flavor to this tasty noodle dish, while the cilantro adds an intense hit of fresh fragrance.

Sesame Noodles with Shrimp & Cilantro

Serves 4

1 garlic clove, chopped

1 scallion, chopped

1 small fresh red chili, seeded and sliced

1 handful fresh cilantro

10½ oz/300 g dried fine egg noodles

2 tbsp vegetable oil

1 tsp shrimp paste

1½ cups raw shelled shrimp

2 tsp sesame oil

2 tbsp lime juice

2 tbsp Thai fish sauce

1 tsp sesame seeds, toasted

Place the garlic, scallion, chili, and cilantro in a mortar and grind with a pestle to a smooth paste.

Bring a large pan of boiling water to a boil. Add the noodles, return to a boil, and cook for 3–4 minutes, or according to the package directions.

Meanwhile, heat the vegetable oil in a preheated wok or large skillet over medium heat. Add the shrimp paste and cilantro mixture and stir-fry for 1 minute.

Add the shrimp and stir-fry for 2 minutes. Stir in the sesame oil, lime juice, and fish sauce and cook for an additional minute.

Drain the noodles, add to the wok, and toss to mix. Sprinkle with the sesame seeds and serve immediately.

Fish & Shellfish

In this sumptuous yet so simple curry, plump, juicy shrimp are perfectly partnered

with sweet–tart fresh pineapple, all bathed in creamy coconut.

Shrimp & Pineapple Curry

serves 4

2 cups coconut cream

½ fresh pineapple, peeled, cored, and chopped

2 tbsp red Thai curry paste

2 tbsp Thai fish sauce

2 tsp sugar

12 oz/350 g raw tiger shrimp, shelled and deveined

2 tbsp chopped fresh cilantro, plus extra, shredded, to garnish

4 scallions, shredded, to garnish

steamed jasmine rice, to serve

Place the coconut cream, pineapple, curry paste, fish sauce, and sugar in a skillet over medium heat. Heat gently until almost boiling. Add the shrimp and cilantro and simmer gently for 3 minutes, or until the shrimp turn pink.

Serve immediately on a bed of steamed jasmine rice, sprinkled with the shredded scallions and cilantro.

The fish in this fragrant, curry-like stew can be varied according to taste or availability, but it's best to stick with those that stay firm when cooked, rather than delicate types that will flake apart too easily.

Spicy Thai Seafood Stew

serves 4

1 lb 2 oz/500 g firm white fish fillets, preferably angler fish or halibut

7 oz/200 g raw squid, cleaned

1 tbsp corn oil

4 shallots, finely chopped

2 garlic cloves, finely chopped

2 tbsp green Thai curry paste

2 small fresh lemon grass stems, finely chopped

1 tsp shrimp paste

2¼ cups coconut milk

7 oz/200 g raw jumbo shrimp, shelled and deveined

12 live clams in their shells, scrubbed

8 fresh Thai or ordinary basil leaves, finely shredded, plus extra sprigs to garnish

boiled rice, to serve

Cut the fish into bite-size chunks and cut the squid body cavities into thick rings.

Heat the oil in a preheated wok or large skillet. Add the shallots, garlic, and curry paste and stir-fry for 1–2 minutes. Add the lemon grass, shrimp paste, and coconut milk and bring to a boil.

Reduce the heat until the liquid is simmering gently, then add the fish, squid, and shrimp to the pan and simmer for 2 minutes.

Add the clams and simmer for 1 minute until the clams have opened. Discard any clams that remain closed.

Serve immediately in individual warmed bowls, spooned over boiled rice, scattered with shredded basil, and garnished with basil sprigs.

Tuna is a firm, meaty-textured fish that is abundant in the seas around Thailand.

You can also use shark or mackerel in this dish.

Sweet-&-Sour Tuna

serves 4

4 fresh tuna steaks, about 1 lb 2 oz/500 g total weight

¼ tsp pepper

2 tbsp peanut oil

1 onion, diced

1 small red bell pepper, seeded and cut into short thin sticks

1 garlic clove, crushed

½ cucumber, seeded and cut into short thin sticks

2 fresh pineapple slices, peeled, cored, and diced

1 tsp finely chopped fresh gingerroot

1 tbsp brown sugar

1 tbsp cornstarch

1½ tbsp lime juice

1 tbsp Thai fish sauce

1 cup fish stock

TO GARNISH

lime slices, halved

cucumber slices

Sprinkle the tuna with the pepper on both sides. Heat a griddle or heavy-bottom skillet over medium–high heat and brush with a little of the oil. Add the tuna and cook for 8 minutes, turning once.

Heat the remaining oil in a separate skillet over medium heat. Add the onion, bell pepper, and garlic and cook, stirring frequently, for 3–4 minutes until softened.

Remove from the heat and stir in the cucumber, pineapple, ginger, and sugar.

Blend the cornstarch with the lime juice and fish sauce, then stir into the stock and add to the skillet. Bring to a boil over medium heat, stirring, then cook for 1–2 minutes until thickened and clear.

Spoon the sauce over the tuna and serve immediately, garnished with halved lime slices and cucumber slices.

The succulence of the salmon flesh and the typical Thai flavorings stay safely locked inside these banana-leaf packages during baking. But don't worry if you can't find banana leaves—use foil or parchment paper instead.

Salmon with Red Curry in Banana Leaves

serves 4

4 salmon steaks, about 6 oz/175 g each

2 banana leaves, halved

1 garlic clove, crushed

1 tsp grated fresh gingerroot

1 tbsp red Thai curry paste

1 tsp brown sugar

1 tbsp Thai fish sauce

2 tbsp lime juice

Preheat the oven to 400°F/200°C.

Place a salmon steak in the center of each banana leaf half. Mix the garlic, ginger, curry paste, sugar, and fish sauce together in a bowl. Spread over both sides of the salmon and sprinkle with the lime juice.

Wrap the banana leaves around the salmon, tucking in the sides as you go, to make a neat package. Seal with wooden toothpicks.

Place the packages, seam-side down, on a cookie sheet and bake in the preheated oven for 15–20 minutes until the fish is cooked and the banana leaves are beginning to brown. Unwrap the packages and serve immediately on individual warmed plates.

The attractive yellow color of these fish fillets comes from the use of turmeric—and

a little goes a long way! If you don't have a steamer, improvise by placing a large

Steamed Yellow Fish Fillets

metal colander over a large pan of boiling water and cover with an upturned

heatproof plate to enclose the fish as it steams.

serves 4

1 lb 2 oz/500 g firm
fish fillets, such as
red snapper, sole,
or angler fish

1 dried bird chili

1 small onion, chopped

3 garlic cloves, chopped

2 fresh cilantro sprigs

1 tsp coriander seeds

½ tsp turmeric

½ tsp pepper

1 tbsp Thai fish sauce

2 tbsp coconut milk

1 small egg, beaten

2 tbsp rice flour

TO SERVE

soy sauce

stir-fried vegetables

Remove any skin from the fish and cut the fillets diagonally into long ¾-inch/2-cm wide strips.

Place the chili, onion, garlic, cilantro, and coriander seeds in a mortar and grind with a pestle to a smooth paste.

Transfer the paste to a bowl and add the turmeric, pepper, fish sauce, coconut milk, and egg. Stir well to mix thoroughly.

Dip the fish strips into the paste mixture, then into the rice flour to coat lightly, shaking off any excess.

Bring the water in the bottom of a steamer to a boil, then arrange the fish strips in the top of the steamer. Cover and steam for 12–15 minutes until the fish is just firm.

Serve the fish immediately with soy sauce and stir-fried vegetables.

Stir-frying is an ideal cooking method for squid as overcooked it can be tough.

It also seals in the natural colors, flavors, and nutritive value of fresh vegetables.

Stir-Fried Squid with Hot Black Bean Sauce

serves 4

1 lb 10 oz/750 g raw squid, cleaned

1 large red bell pepper, seeded

1 cup snow peas

1 head bok choy

3 tbsp black bean sauce

1 tbsp Thai fish sauce

1 tbsp rice wine

1 tbsp dark soy sauce

1 tsp brown sugar

1 tsp cornstarch

1 tbsp water

1 tbsp corn oil

1 tsp sesame oil

1 small Thai chili, chopped

1 garlic clove, finely chopped

1 tsp grated fresh gingerroot

2 scallions, chopped

Cut the tentacles from the squid and discard. Cut the body cavities into quarters lengthwise. Use the tip of a small, sharp knife to score a diamond pattern in the flesh, without cutting all the way through. Pat dry with paper towels.

Cut the bell pepper into long, thin slices. Cut the snow peas in half diagonally. Coarsely shred the bok choy.

Mix the black bean sauce, fish sauce, rice wine, soy sauce, and sugar together in a small bowl. Blend the cornstarch with the water and stir into the other sauce ingredients. Set aside.

Heat the oils in a preheated wok or large skillet over high heat. Add the chili, garlic, ginger, and scallions and stir-fry for 1 minute. Add the bell pepper and stir-fry for 2 minutes.

Add the squid and stir-fry for 1 minute. Stir in the snow peas and bok choy and stir-fry for 1 minute, or until the bok choy is just wilted.

Stir in the sauce ingredients and cook, stirring, for 2 minutes, or until the sauce clears and thickens. Serve immediately.

Lemon grass, galangal, and lime leaves delicately flavor and perfume this simple and elegant dish. Serve with a chili sauce for dipping, if you like.

Thai Fragrant Mussels

serves 4

4 lb 8 oz/2 kg live mussels

2 fresh lemon grass stems, bruised

2-inch/5-cm piece fresh galangal or gingerroot, bruised

5 fresh kaffir lime leaves, shredded

3 garlic cloves

1¼ cups water

salt

Clean the mussels by scrubbing or scraping the shells and pulling out any beards that are attached to them. Discard any with broken shells or any that refuse to close when tapped.

Place the mussels, lemon grass, galangal, lime leaves, garlic, and water in a large, heavy-bottom pan or flameproof casserole and season to taste with salt. Bring to a boil, then cover and cook over high heat, shaking the pan occasionally, for 5 minutes, or until the mussels have opened.

Remove and discard the flavorings and any mussels that remain closed. Divide the mussels between 4 warmed soup bowls with a slotted spoon. Tilt the pan and let any sand settle, then spoon the cooking liquid over the mussels and serve immediately.

Meat & Poultry

A quick-and-easy stir-fry for any day of the week, this simple beef recipe is a good

one-pan main dish. Serve with a crisp green side salad to complete the meal.

Stir-Fried Beef with Bean Sprouts

serves 4

1 bunch scallions

2 tbsp corn oil

1 garlic clove, crushed

1 tsp finely chopped fresh gingerroot

1 lb 2 oz/500 g lean beef tenderloin, cut into thin strips

1 large red bell pepper, seeded and sliced

1 small fresh red chili, seeded and chopped

3 cups fresh bean sprouts

1 small fresh lemon grass stem, finely chopped

2 tbsp smooth peanut butter

4 tbsp coconut milk

1 tbsp rice vinegar

1 tbsp soy sauce

1 tsp brown sugar

9 oz/250 g dried medium egg noodles

salt and pepper

Trim and thinly slice the scallions, setting aside some slices to use as a garnish.

Heat the oil in a preheated wok or large skillet over high heat. Add the scallions, garlic, and ginger and stir-fry for 2–3 minutes. Add the beef and stir-fry for 4–5 minutes until browned all over.

Add the bell pepper and stir-fry for 3–4 minutes. Add the chili and bean sprouts and stir-fry for 2 minutes. Mix the lemon grass, peanut butter, coconut milk, vinegar, soy sauce, and sugar together in a bowl, then stir into the wok.

Meanwhile, bring a large pan of lightly salted water to a boil. Add the noodles, return to a boil, and cook for 4 minutes, or according to the package directions. Drain, stir into the wok, and toss to mix.

Season to taste with salt and pepper, if necessary. Sprinkle with the reserved scallions and serve immediately.

meat & poultry

A delicately flavored stir-fry infused with lemon grass and ginger, with bell peppers

adding color and texture. Cutting the beef across the grain ensures tenderness.

Beef, Bell Peppers & Lemon Grass

serves 4

1 lb 2 oz/500 g lean
beef tenderloin

2 tbsp vegetable oil

1 garlic clove, finely
chopped

1 fresh lemon grass
stem, finely shredded

1-inch/2.5-cm piece
fresh gingerroot, finely
chopped

1 red bell pepper,
seeded and thickly sliced

1 green bell pepper,
seeded and thickly sliced

1 onion, thickly sliced

2 tbsp lime juice

boiled noodles or rice,
to serve

Cut the beef into long, thin strips across the grain.

Heat the oil in a preheated wok or large skillet over high heat. Add the garlic and stir-fry for 1 minute.

Add the beef and stir-fry for 2–3 minutes until lightly colored. Stir in the lemon grass and ginger and remove the pan from the heat.

Remove the beef from the pan with a slotted spoon and set aside. Add the bell peppers and onion to the pan and stir-fry over high heat for 2–3 minutes until the onions are just turning golden brown and are slightly softened.

Return the beef to the pan, stir in the lime juice, and season to taste with salt and pepper. Heat through briefly, then serve immediately with boiled noodles or rice.

Sweetly perfumed mango adds an exotic

dimension to this chicken and vegetable stir-fry

—ideal for an uplifting midweek family meal.

Chicken & Mango Stir-Fry

serves 4

6 skinless, boneless chicken thighs

1-inch/2.5-cm piece fresh gingerroot, peeled and grated

1 garlic clove, crushed

1 small fresh red chili, seeded

1 large red bell pepper, seeded

4 scallions

1½ cups snow peas

1 cup baby corn

1 large firm, ripe mango

2 tbsp corn oil

1 tbsp light soy sauce

3 tbsp rice wine or sherry

1 tsp sesame oil

salt and pepper

Cut the chicken into long, thin strips and place in a bowl. Mix the ginger, garlic, and chili together, then stir into the chicken strips to coat evenly.

Thinly slice the bell pepper diagonally. Diagonally slice the scallions. Cut the snow peas and corn in half diagonally. Peel the mango, remove and discard the pit, and thinly slice the flesh.

Heat the corn oil in a preheated wok or large skillet over high heat. Add the chicken and stir-fry for 4–5 minutes until just turning golden brown. Add the bell peppers and stir-fry over medium heat for 4–5 minutes until softened. Add the scallions, snow peas, and corn and stir-fry for 1 minute.

Mix the soy sauce, rice wine, and sesame oil together in a small bowl and stir into the wok. Add the mango and stir gently for 1 minute until heated through. Season to taste with salt and pepper, if necessary, and serve immediately.

meat & poultry

This classic green Thai curry, full of sharp, fresh flavor and enriched with coconut cream, is simplicity itself to prepare using ready-made curry paste.

Quick Green Chicken Curry

serves 4

1 tbsp vegetable oil

6 scallions, sliced

1 lb 5 oz/600 g skinless, boneless chicken breast, cut into cubes

scant 1 cup coconut cream

3 tbsp green Thai curry paste

3 tbsp chopped fresh cilantro

boiled noodles or rice, to serve

Heat the oil in a preheated wok or large skillet over high heat. Add the scallions and chicken and stir-fry for 3–4 minutes until the chicken is lightly colored.

Stir in the coconut cream and curry paste and cook for an additional 5 minutes, or until the chicken is cooked through. Add a little water or stock if the sauce becomes too thick.

Stir in the cilantro and serve immediately with boiled noodles or rice.

The addition of three different colors of bell pepper makes this stir-fry wonderfully

vibrant, while the chili sauce and oil give it a fiery kick.

Pork with Bell Peppers

serves 4

1 tbsp vegetable or peanut oil

1 tbsp chili oil

1 lb/450 g pork fillet, thinly sliced

2 tbsp green chili sauce

6 scallions, sliced

1-inch/2.5-cm piece fresh gingerroot, peeled and thinly sliced

1 red bell pepper, seeded and sliced

1 yellow bell pepper, seeded and sliced

1 orange bell pepper, seeded and sliced

1 tbsp Thai fish sauce

2 tbsp soy sauce

juice of ½ lime

4 tbsp chopped fresh flat-leaf parsley

cooked rice stick noodles, to serve

Heat the oils in a preheated wok or large skillet over high heat. Add the pork, in batches, and stir-fry until browned all over.

Remove from the pan with a slotted spoon and set aside.

Add the chili sauce, scallions, and ginger to the pan and stir-fry for 1–2 minutes. Add the bell peppers and stir–fry for 2–3 minutes.

Return the pork to the pan, stir well, and add the fish sauce, soy sauce, and lime juice. Cook for an additional 1–2 minutes, then stir in the parsley. Serve immediately with cooked rice stick noodles.

meat & poultry

Tamarind, which comes from the pods of a tree of the pea family, adds a unique

fruity sourness to Asian dishes, and marries particularly well with pork.

Tamarind Pork

serves 4

2 tbsp vegetable oil

1 lb 5 oz/600 g pork fillet, cut into thin strips

8 oz/225 g canned bamboo shoots, drained and rinsed

boiled noodles, to serve

SPICE PASTE

4 shallots, finely chopped

2 garlic cloves, finely chopped

1-inch/2.5-cm piece fresh gingerroot, peeled and finely chopped

1 tsp ground coriander

2 fresh red chilies, seeded and finely chopped

1/2 tsp turmeric

6 whole blanched almonds, finely chopped

2 tbsp tamarind paste

2 tbsp hot water

To make the spice paste, place all the spice paste ingredients in a blender or food processor and process until smooth. Set aside.

Heat the oil in a preheated wok or large skillet over high heat. Add the pork and stir-fry for 3 minutes, or until the meat is lightly colored. Add the spice paste and stir-fry for 2–3 minutes.

Add the bamboo shoots and stir-fry for an additional 2 minutes, or until the pork is cooked through. Serve immediately, spooned over boiled noodles.

This warmly spiced, ultra-quick dish makes a great family meal. Just cook fine egg noodles for an accompaniment while the meat sizzles.

Spicy Fried Ground Pork

serves 4

2 tbsp corn oil

2 garlic cloves, finely chopped

3 shallots, finely chopped

1-inch/2.5-cm piece fresh gingerroot, peeled and finely chopped

1 lb 2 oz/500 g lean ground pork

2 tbsp Thai fish sauce

1 tbsp dark soy sauce

1 tbsp red Thai curry paste

4 dried kaffir lime leaves, crumbled

4 plum tomatoes, chopped

3 tbsp chopped fresh cilantro, plus extra sprigs to garnish

salt and pepper

boiled fine egg noodles, to serve

Heat the oil in a preheated wok or large skillet over medium heat. Add the garlic, shallots, and ginger and stir-fry for 2 minutes. Stir in the pork and stir-fry until browned.

Stir in the fish sauce, soy sauce, curry paste, and lime leaves, and stir-fry for 1–2 minutes over high heat.

Add the tomatoes and cook, stirring occasionally, for an additional 5–6 minutes.

Stir in the chopped cilantro and season to taste with salt and pepper. Serve hot, spooned over boiled fine egg noodles and garnished with cilantro sprigs.

A speedy dish, typical of Thai street food. This includes fresh corn, which, although

introduced relatively recently to Thailand, is a very popular vegetable used in many

Stir-Fried Pork & Corn

dishes. Kernels cut from corncobs, the fresher the better, is first choice, but if not

available, use drained, canned corn kernels instead.

serves 4

2 tbsp vegetable oil

1 lb 2 oz/500 g pork fillet, cut into thin strips

1 garlic clove, chopped

2 cups fresh corn kernels

1½ cups green beans, cut into short lengths

2 scallions, chopped

1 small fresh red chili, chopped

1 tsp sugar

1 tbsp light soy sauce

3 tbsp chopped fresh cilantro

boiled egg noodles or rice, to serve

Heat the oil in a preheated wok or large skillet over high heat. Add the pork and stir-fry until browned all over.

Stir in the garlic, corn, beans, scallions, and chili and stir-fry for 2–3 minutes.

Stir in the sugar and soy sauce and stir-fry for 30 seconds.

Sprinkle with the cilantro and serve immediately with boiled egg noodles or rice.

Vegetables & Salads

These crisp, delicately preserved vegetables are usually served as an accompaniment to fried meat or fish dishes.

Crisp Pickled Vegetables

serves 6–8

½ small cauliflower

½ cucumber, seeded

7 oz/200 g green beans

½ small head Napa cabbage

2 carrots, peeled

2¼ cups rice vinegar

1 tbsp sugar

1 tsp salt

3 garlic cloves

3 shallots

3 Thai chilies

5 tbsp peanut oil

Cut all the vegetables into bite-sized pieces. If you have time, cut the carrots into flower shapes.

Place the vinegar, sugar, and salt in a large pan and bring almost to a boil. Add the beans, cabbage, and carrot and reduce the heat and simmer for 3–4 minutes until just tender but still crisp inside. Remove the pan from the heat and let the vegetables and vinegar cool.

Meanwhile, peel the garlic and shallots and seed the chilies. Place in a mortar and grind with a pestle to a smooth paste.

Heat the oil in a preheated wok or large skillet over medium heat. Add the garlic and shallot paste and stir-fry for 1–2 minutes. Add the vegetables with the vinegar and cook, stirring, for 2 minutes, or until the liquid is reduced slightly. Remove from the heat and let cool.

Serve the pickles cold, or pack into sterilized jars and store in the refrigerator for up to 2 weeks.

vegetables & salads

This interesting dish, which features succulent mushrooms filled with crispy

vegetables and tofu, makes a great vegetarian entrée. Serve it with a fresh salad.

Thai-Spiced Mushrooms

serves 4

8 large, flat mushrooms

3 tbsp corn oil

2 tbsp light soy sauce

1 garlic clove, crushed

¾-inch/2-cm piece fresh galangal or gingerroot, peeled and grated

1 tbsp green Thai curry paste

8 baby corn, sliced

3 scallions, chopped

generous 1 cup fresh bean sprouts

3½ oz/100 g firm tofu (drained weight), diced

2 tsp sesame seeds, toasted

Remove the stems from the mushrooms and set aside. Place the caps on a cookie sheet. Mix 2 tablespoons of the oil with 1 tablespoon of the soy sauce and brush over the mushrooms. Cook under a broiler preheated to high until golden and tender, turning once.

Meanwhile, finely chop the mushroom stems. Heat the remaining oil in a preheated wok or large skillet over high heat. Add the mushroom stems, garlic, and galangal and stir-fry for 1 minute. Stir in the curry paste, corn, and scallions and stir-fry for 1 minute. Add the bean sprouts and stir-fry for 1 minute.

Add the tofu and remaining soy sauce, then toss lightly until heated through. Spoon the mixture into the mushroom caps.

Sprinkle with the sesame seeds and serve immediately.

The "red" in the title refers not to the beans but to the sauce, which has a warm,

rusty color. This is a lively way not only to serve fresh green beans but to lift the

flavor of frozen beans, too.

Thai Red Bean Curry

serves 4

14 oz/400 g green beans

1 garlic clove, finely sliced

1 Thai chili, seeded and chopped

1/2 tsp paprika

1 fresh lemon grass stem, finely chopped

2 tsp Thai fish sauce

1/2 cup coconut milk

1 tbsp corn oil

2 scallions, sliced

Cut the beans into 2-inch/5-cm pieces. Bring a pan of water to a boil. Add the beans, return to a boil, and cook for 2 minutes. Drain well.

Place the garlic, chili, paprika, lemon grass, fish sauce, and coconut milk in a blender or food processor and process to a smooth paste.

Heat the oil in a preheated wok or large skillet over high heat. Add the scallions and stir-fry for 1 minute. Add the spice paste and bring to a boil.

Simmer for 3–4 minutes until reduced by about half. Add the beans and simmer for an additional 1–2 minutes until tender. Transfer to a warmed serving bowl and serve immediately.

Tempting cubes of golden fried tofu and colorful carrot and bell peppers are anointed with a hot–sweet sauce to make a substantial side dish or light lunch dish.

Crispy Tofu with Chili Soy Sauce

serves 4

10½ oz/300 g firm tofu (drained weight)

2 tbsp vegetable oil

1 garlic clove, sliced

1 carrot, cut into short thin sticks

½ green bell pepper, seeded and cut into short thin sticks

1 Thai chili, seeded and finely chopped

2 tbsp soy sauce

1 tbsp lime juice

1 tbsp Thai fish sauce

1 tbsp brown sugar

pickled ginger slices, to serve (optional)

Pat the tofu dry with paper towels. Cut into ¾-inch/2-cm cubes.

Heat the oil in a preheated wok or large skillet over high heat. Add the garlic and stir-fry for 1 minute. Remove the garlic with a slotted spoon and set aside. Add the tofu and cook, turning gently, until well browned all over.

Remove the tofu with a slotted spoon, drain on paper towels, and keep warm. Add the carrot and bell peppers to the pan and stir-fry for 1 minute.

Pile the tofu into a serving dish and spoon the carrot and bell peppers on top.

Mix the chili, soy sauce, lime juice, fish sauce, and sugar together in a bowl, stirring until the sugar has dissolved. Spoon over the tofu mixture and serve topped with the reserved garlic slices and pickled ginger slices, if desired.

This composition of rice noodles and shrimp,

lightly dressed with Thai flavors, makes an

impressive first course or a light lunch.

Thai Noodle & Shrimp Salad

serves 4

3 oz/85 g fine rice noodles

6 oz/175 g snow peas, halved crosswise if large

5 tbsp lime juice

4 tbsp Thai fish sauce

1 tbsp sugar, or to taste

1-inch/2.5-cm piece fresh gingerroot, peeled and finely chopped

1 fresh red chili, seeded and thinly sliced diagonally

4 tbsp chopped fresh cilantro or mint, plus extra to garnish

4-inch/10-cm piece cucumber, peeled, seeded, and diced

2 scallions, thinly sliced diagonally

20–24 large cooked shrimp, shelled and deveined but 4 reserved in their shells to garnish

2 tbsp toasted chopped unsalted peanuts (optional)

lemon slices, to garnish

Soak the noodles in a bowl of hot water for 5 minutes, or according to the package directions. Drain, rinse under cold running water until cold, then drain again. Set aside.

Bring a pan of water to a boil. Add the snow peas, return to a boil, and cook for 1 minute. Drain, rinse under cold running water until cold, then drain again. Set aside.

Whisk the lime juice, fish sauce, sugar, ginger, chili, and chopped cilantro together in a large bowl. Stir in the cucumber and scallions, then add the noodles, snow peas, and shelled shrimp. Toss the salad gently to combine.

Divide the salad between 4 large plates. Sprinkle with peanuts, if using, and extra chopped cilantro, then garnish each plate with a shrimp in its shell, lemon slice, and cilantro sprig. Serve immediately.

vegetables & salads

Bok choy, also called pak choi or Chinese chard, has a delicate, fresh flavor and crisp texture, which is best retained by light, quick cooking. This makes it an ideal choice for stir-frying.

Bok Choy with Crabmeat

serves 4

2 heads green bok choy, about 9 oz/250 g total weight

2 tbsp vegetable oil

1 garlic clove, thinly sliced

2 tbsp oyster sauce

1 cup cherry tomatoes, halved

6 oz/175 g canned white crabmeat, drained

salt and pepper

Trim the bok choy and cut into 1-inch/2.5-cm thick slices.

Heat the oil in a preheated wok or large skillet over high heat. Add the garlic and stir-fry for 1 minute.

Add the bok choy and stir-fry for 2–3 minutes until the leaves are just wilted but the stems are still crisp.

Add the oyster sauce and tomatoes and stir-fry for 1 minute. Add the crabmeat and salt and pepper to taste and stir-fry for 1–2 minutes until heated through. Serve immediately.

An unusual side salad that is a good accompaniment to any simple Thai entrée, especially broiled meats and fish. Add the dressing just before serving or the leaves will lose their desirable crispness.

Thai Green Salad

serves 4–6

1 small head romaine lettuce

1 bunch scallions

½ cucumber

4 tbsp coarsely shredded fresh coconut, toasted

DRESSING

4 tbsp lime juice

2 tbsp Thai fish sauce

1 small Thai chili, finely chopped

1 tsp sugar

1 garlic clove, crushed

2 tbsp chopped fresh cilantro

1 tbsp chopped fresh mint

Tear or coarsely shred the lettuce and place in a large salad bowl.

Trim and thinly slice the scallions diagonally and add to the bowl.

Use a vegetable peeler to shave thin slices along the length of the cucumber and add to the bowl.

Place all the dressing ingredients in a screw-top jar, screw the lid on tightly, and shake well to blend thoroughly.

Pour the dressing over the salad and toss well to coat the leaves evenly. Scatter the coconut over the salad and toss in lightly just before serving.

This is a luxurious salad, featuring cooked fresh seafood, complemented by clean, zesty flavorings—ideal for a summery lunch al fresco.

Mixed Seafood Salad

serves 4

1 lb/450 g live mussels

3 tbsp vegetable or peanut oil

1 small onion, thinly sliced

8 oz/225 g raw baby squid, cleaned and sliced

8 oz/225 g cooked shelled shrimp

1 bunch scallions, coarsely chopped

1 fresh lemon grass stem, finely chopped

1 red bell pepper, seeded and cut into strips

½ small head Napa cabbage, shredded

2 garlic cloves, crushed

1 tsp Thai fish sauce

1 tsp jaggery or brown sugar

juice of 1 lemon

2-inch/5-cm piece cucumber, chopped

1 tomato, seeded and chopped

Clean the mussels by scrubbing or scraping the shells and pulling out any beards that are attached to them. Discard any with broken shells or any that refuse to close when tapped.

Heat 1 tablespoon of the oil in a preheated wok or large skillet over high heat. Add the onion, squid, shrimp, and mussels and stir-fry for 1–2 minutes, until the squid is opaque and the mussels have opened. Discard any mussels that remain closed.

Mix the scallions, lemon grass, bell pepper, and Napa cabbage together in a bowl. Add the seafood and stir gently to mix. Turn into a serving dish.

Mix the garlic, the remaining oil, fish sauce, sugar, and lemon juice together in a small bowl. Add the cucumber and tomato to the dressing, spoon over the salad and seafood, and serve immediately.

This recipe makes a good accompaniment for spicy broiled fish and meat dishes.

Once made, it can be chilled with the dressing for 1–2 hours, but is best eaten on

the day of making.

Cucumber Salad

serves 4

1 cucumber

1 tsp salt

1 small red onion

1 garlic clove, crushed

½ tsp chili paste

2 tsp Thai fish sauce

1 tbsp lime juice

1 tsp sesame oil

Trim the cucumber and coarsely grate the flesh. Place in a colander over a bowl, sprinkle with the salt, and let drain for 20 minutes. Transfer the cucumber flesh to a bowl, discarding the liquid.

Peel the onion and finely chop, then toss into the cucumber. Spoon into 4 individual bowls or 1 large one.

Mix the garlic, chili paste, fish sauce, lime juice, and oil together in a separate bowl, then spoon over the salad. Cover and chill in the refrigerator before serving.

Desserts

These inviting individual creamy coconut desserts are exotically flavored with

perfumed rose water. Serve with a colorful selection of fresh fruits.

Coconut Cream Custard

serves 4

4 large eggs

**generous ½ cup
superfine sugar**

**scant 1 cup coconut
cream**

1 tbsp rose water

fresh fruits, to serve

Preheat the oven to 350°F/180°C.

Beat the eggs, sugar, coconut cream, and rose water together in a bowl until the sugar has dissolved.

Divide the custard mixture between 4 ramekins. Place in a roasting pan and pour in boiling water to come halfway up the sides of the ramekins. Bake in the preheated oven for 20–30 minutes, or until set. Remove from the pan and let cool.

To turn out, run a sharp knife around the edge of each custard and turn out onto a serving dish. Serve with fresh fruits.

This irresistible, classic Thai dessert is best served with a squeeze of lime juice and topped with a generous spoonful of vanilla ice cream.

Banana Fritters in Coconut Batter

serves 4

9 tbsp all-purpose flour

2 tbsp rice flour

1 tbsp superfine sugar

1 egg, separated

⅔ cup coconut milk

4 large bananas

corn oil, for deep-frying

TO DECORATE

1 tsp confectioners' sugar

1 tsp ground cinnamon

Sift the all-purpose flour, rice flour, and superfine sugar into a bowl and make a well in the center. Add the egg yolk and coconut milk to the well and gradually beat in the dry ingredients until a smooth, thick batter forms.

Whisk the egg white in a separate clean, dry, greasefree bowl until stiff enough to hold soft peaks. Lightly fold into the batter.

Heat a 2½-inch/6-cm depth of oil in a large pan to 350–375°F/ 180–190°C, or until a cube of bread browns in 30 seconds. Peel the bananas, then cut in half crosswise. Dip quickly into the batter to coat. Deep-fry, in batches, for 2–3 minutes until golden brown, turning once.

Drain well on paper towels. Sprinkle with confectioners' sugar and cinnamon and serve immediately.

desserts

What could be more comforting than morsels of melting banana coated in a sweet coconut milk sauce? You could use jaggery or brown sugar instead of white sugar.

Thai Bananas

serves 6

1½ cups coconut milk

2 tbsp granulated sugar

½ tsp salt

6 slightly underripe bananas, peeled and cut into 2-inch/5-cm lengths

1 tbsp sesame seeds, toasted, to decorate

Place the coconut milk, sugar, and salt in a pan over low heat and heat, stirring, until the sugar has dissolved. Add the banana pieces and cook for 5 minutes, or until the bananas are soft but not mushy.

Divide the banana mixture between 6 small bowls. Scatter the sesame seeds over and serve immediately.

These crêpes are made with coconut milk for a special Thai twist. Try banana and mango as an alternative filling and decorate with toasted shredded coconut.

Thai Crêpes with Papaya & Passion Fruit

serves 4

2 eggs

½ cup coconut milk

¾ cup milk

1 cup all-purpose flour

½ tsp salt

1 tbsp superfine sugar

1 tbsp butter, melted

vegetable oil, for pan-frying

sifted confectioners' sugar, for dusting

FILLING

2 papayas

3 passion fruits

juice of 1 lime

2 tbsp confectioners' sugar

Whisk the eggs, coconut milk, and milk together in a bowl. Sift the flour and salt into a separate large bowl, stir in the superfine sugar, and make a well in the center. Add the egg mixture to the well and gradually beat in the dry ingredients until a smooth, thick batter forms. Stir in the melted butter.

Heat an 8–9-inch/20–23-cm nonstick skillet over medium–high heat and brush with oil. Pour in enough batter to coat the bottom of the skillet—tip the skillet as you pour it in, so that the bottom is evenly coated. Cook until browned on the underside and set on top, then turn the crêpe over and cook the other side. Transfer to a warmed plate, cover with foil, and keep warm while making the remaining crêpes.

Peel the papayas and cut in half, then scoop out and discard the seeds, reserving a few for a garnish. Cut the flesh into chunks and place in a bowl. Cut the passion fruits in half, then scoop the seeds and pulp into the bowl. Stir in the lime juice and confectioners' sugar. Place a little filling on 1 quarter of each crêpe. Fold in half, then into quarters. Dust with sifted confectioners' sugar. Scatter over the reserved papaya seeds and serve immediately.

desserts

This elegant fruit salad would provide a light, refreshing finale to any Thai meal.

Make in advance and let the salad stand so the flavors blend and develop.

Thai Mixed Fruit Salad (Polamai Ruam)

serves 4

1 papaya, halved, peeled, and seeded

2 bananas, peeled and thickly sliced

1 small fresh pineapple, peeled, halved, cored, and sliced

12 fresh litchis, peeled

1 small melon, seeded and cut into thin wedges

2 oranges

grated rind and juice of 1 lime

2 tbsp superfine sugar

Arrange the papaya, bananas, pineapple, litchis, and melon in a shallow serving dish. Cut the rind and white pith from the oranges. Cut the orange slices from between the membranes and add to the other fruits. Grate a small quantity of the discarded orange rind and scatter over the fruits.

Mix the lime rind and juice and sugar together in a small bowl, stirring until the sugar has dissolved. Pour over the salad, toss gently to coat, and serve.

Index